BE RECORDER

ALSO BY CARMEN GIMÉNEZ SMITH

Cruel Futures

Angels of the Americlypse: An Anthology of New Latin@ Writing
(with John Chávez)

Milk and Filth

Goodbye, Flicker

The City She Was

Can We Talk Here

Reason's Monster

Bring Down the Little Birds: On Mothering, Art, Work, and Everything Else

Odalisque in Pieces

BE RECORDER

poems

Carmen Giménez Smith

Graywolf Press

This publication is made possible, in part, by the voters of Minnesota through a Minnesota State Arts Board Operating Support grant, thanks to a legislative appropriation from the arts and cultural heritage fund. Significant support has also been provided by Target, the McKnight Foundation, the Lannan Foundation, the Amazon Literary Partnership, and other generous contributions from foundations, corporations, and individuals. To these organizations and individuals we offer our heartfelt thanks.

Published by Graywolf Press
250 Third Avenue North, Suite 600
Minneapolis, Minnesota 55401

www.graywolfpress.org

Published in the United States of America

ISBN 978-1-55597-848-8

2 4 6 8 10 9 7 5 3

Library of Congress Control Number: 2018958160

Cover design: Mary Austin Speaker

Cover art: Daniel Martin Diaz

For Mark Wunderlich

CONTENTS

ONE: Creation Myth

    ORIGINS • 3

    WATCH WHAT HAPPENS • 4

    BOY CRAZY • 5

    PLAY THERAPY • 6

    SELF AS DEEP AS COMA • 7

    SOUTHERN CONE • 9

    CURRENT AFFAIRS • 10

    INTERVIEW FOLLOW-UP • 11

    NO APOLOGY: A POEMIFESTO • 12

    FLAT EARTH DREAM SOLILOQUY • 13

TWO: Be Recorder

    BE RECORDER • 17

THREE: Birthright

    IN REMEMBRANCE OF THEIR LABORS • 63

    AS BODY II • 65

    I WILL BE MY MOTHER'S APPRENTICE • 67

    BEASTS • 68

    ENTANGLEMENT • 70

    AMERICAN MYTHOS • 71

    ON TEACHING • 76

    TERMINAL HAIR • 77

    ONLY A SHADOW • 78

    ARS POETICA • 79

NOTES • 81

ACKNOWLEDGMENTS • 83

Gracias a la vida que me ha dado tanto
Me ha dado el sonido y el abecedario

Violeta Parra

ONE • Creation Myth

ORIGINS

People sometimes confuse me for someone else they know
because they've projected an idea onto me. I've developed
a second sense for this—some call it paranoia, but I call it
the profoundest consciousness on the face of the earth.
This gift was passed on to me from my mother who learned it from
solid and socially constructed doors whooshing inches from her face.
It may seem like a lie to anyone who has not felt the whoosh, but
a door swinging inches from your face is no joke. It feels like being
invisible, which is also what it feels like when someone looks
at your face and thinks you're someone else. In graduate school
a teacher called me by another woman's name with not even
brown skin, but what you might call a brown name. That sting
took years to overcome, but I got over it and here
I am with a name that's at the front of this object, a name
I've made singular, that I spent my whole life making.

WATCH WHAT HAPPENS

The housewives on television and their bottles
of wine—whose corks laid in a single row
would circumnavigate three complete orbits
around the sun—are only teaching us how hard
the human zoo of the middle class can be.
We have organic and TV and Spanx and TV
and kale and açai and also pills for penises to get even
harder. TV. And Toyotas and Febreze and Blue Apron.
The housewives nitpick their daughters, throw drinks
we won't, blackball the mean mom we wish we could.
Meanwhile, we aspire to live in houses that mansiony
and to live through our daughters and we
tear down other women's faces and husbands
and poor choices, quietly because we're not paid
or rewarded to and could face criminal or civil action.
If I were a reality TV actress, maybe in my 60s
and I had changed my face, and the old face haunted
me or if, as I got older, maybe 72, I wanted to see
what it would look like if I had remained the original face,
I would pitch a new show called *Back in Time*, which
would chronicle my return to the invisibility of civilian life.

BOY CRAZY

The echoes of sirens and cicadas,
and the drunk boys who howl
into the trees at 2 a.m. infect
my window while I sleep,
and I'm pulled into a girl I once was,
calling for love into a sky transected
by power lines until sunrise when the town
tightened into itself. I prayed for a boy's
wolf life, the dream of skulking along
streets with hunger and immunity.
I wanted to cup the moon's curve
in my hand like it belonged to me,
that was how young I was.

PLAY THERAPY

I am the puppet a girl flops around in her dollhouse,
and I represent her anger. I'm daughter and teacher
and cousin too. I'm brother and Papa Smurf is baby.
The girl's made a ratty mattress from a red quilt patch.
The pillow is a dirty cotton ball where I reenact the scene
of her father (Ken) weeping into her breasts. Then
she pulls the arms off of him, then I stop being her
and go down to the kitchen to be a mother who is quiet,
and martyred, and the both of us make meals
from our symbiotic tragedy. I've 3,000 roles
in the air ready for the girl's next endeavor. In the next
room, this girl becomes a poet, both brilliant and mean.

SELF AS DEEP AS COMA

When I was a girl, I thought clouds were God,
and that we dialogued about sin,
which mirrored my desires. When our talks
made me paranoid, I counted the letters
in each word I heard, turned them backward
or rearranged them alphabetically to dodge
the buzz of my head. Other times
I was the satyr side of the coin and the air
around me felt like jewels.
Then abyss. Pulling the hair
from my head and a type of catatonia.
My family thought I should lift myself
with mind, lift myself
from the bed, from the couch, as if the body
were the mind's queen. We've seen
the world, my family would tell me. In the world
suffering is hunger, war, disease, they said,
and because those calamities were terrible,
I was ashamed for the insignificance of mine.
What I had I had made, they said,
and I should cast it off like a snake molting skin,
so I would try, each of my atoms a ton,
which led to a thought experiment at eleven, death
by pills. I survived, woozy but alive. No scar left,
no redemption or courage, just shame so dark
my ancestors called from the fathoms
to ask why I sought out their shadows.

To end a conversation, tell a story of suicide
with a girl in it. She's a ghost desperate for absolution.
When I was a girl, I wilted or blew. I burrowed into pain.
When I was a girl, I thought my storm would suck me
into its eye and uncoil me from what I was.

When I was a girl, I worried about who knew I knew.
I worried who I could hurt, so I hid myself.

We are storms and bargains
with heaven, pulses of electricity moving
within infinite networks.
So much fallibility. What do we bear
that comes just from the world?
And then what comes from inside us?
We bear everything. Each part.

I loved the part when the world was
my torrid lover seduced by the blue blaze
beaming from my body. My eye helped me
plow through the living room like a comet.
I could burn down or out or err,
and I could be such a good poet in it
sometimes. I liked how brilliant
the light words emitted, stars I arranged
in a sky like a god who would fall to the earth
having made something beautiful and vainglorious.
Sometimes those were the days, the ones
I could hold still long enough to arrange
stars without the burn. But I cannot.
I have in me a buried spark. I buried it myself.

When I was a girl, I collected reams of paper, soothed
by the white over and over, the hope of starting
from blank. I hoped to endure being well enough,
to conjure a new bright vessel because I wanted to live.

SOUTHERN CONE

I wept with my grandmother when Reagan
was shot because that's what she wanted.
At night, she'd tell me about a city built
by Evita for children in Buenos Aires, the city
of her first exile. Children went about
municipal duties in the small post office
and mini city hall to learn to be good citizens.
In Argentina she sold bread pudding
and gave French and English lessons from her
home for money to buy shoes. She promised
we'd go someday, but we never did. She'd say
Peruvians were gossipy, Argentinians snobbish, but
Chileans were above reproach. A little bit migrant,
a little bit food insecurity, she was the brass bust
of JFK on her altar, the holy card of Saint Anthony
on her TV. She was her green card and the ebony cross
above her bed. The lilted yes when she answered
the phone, and the song she liked to hum about bells
and God that ended tirin-tin-tin-tirin-tin-tan: miles
and ages away from her story, she sang it.

CURRENT AFFAIRS

A mob slid like protozoa
across the palace plaza,
a Greek choral malignancy,
treacly and pulsing while
a cannon sponsored by Red
Bull shot out T-shirts
with GPS tracking in the *Make
America Great Again* stitching.
We screamed yasssssssss
for a decade and that is
what had happened.

INTERVIEW FOLLOW-UP

I'm a very hard worker, so how much
will you pay to tuck me into your
pocket? My qualifications are that
I am an immigrant mother once removed thus
motivated to ruthlessly carry my babies to the top.
I resign myself to this mortification
for passage into the Amazon marketplace
with my good people skills and killer drive.
Available immediately. Fine print: you can own
my labor, but not my defiance. You can shape
my toil into a robot with nearly real skin,
but you can't touch the feeble efforts I make to retaliate.

NO APOLOGY: A POEMIFESTO

Isn't there a line by Yusef Komunyakaa, "I apologize for the eyes
in my head." Maybe what I am trying to say is that I apologize
for the sight in my eyes. Susan Briante

I would love to make a proposal, and it is out of love,
not patronizing love but true revolutionary love, and it won't
upset the orbit tomorrow. So here's where I'd like
to begin, and this might be the hardest thing you've tried to do,
or maybe you already do it and I'm grateful for you
because you've inspired me. I know it's the hardest thing
for me because I haven't done it consistently (not at all, sorry),
but I want to recommend that we stop apologizing.
Today I counted and I said I'm sorry approximately 22 times.
I apologized for my setting my stuff down on the counter at Kroger.
I apologized for being behind someone at a copy machine.
I apologized for someone else bumping into a stranger.
I apologized for taking longer than a minute to explain an idea.
Suffice it to say I am sorry all the time.
I won't tell you what to do because that makes me
an implicit solicitor of sorry. Personally,
when the word comes into my mouth, I'm going to shape it into
a seed to plant in another woman's aura as love. I only ask
that we get started. This is our first step toward world domination.

FLAT EARTH DREAM SOLILOQUY

I like the skeptical credo of Flat Earth—the bits about reinventing knowledge, but I hate the part about borders and brutalism. With a photo of the horizon taken from a plane and Photoshop you can swarm science with swagger. A Flat Earth makes water endless, and any talk of hardship is theater, and it will never let us down, and drinking urine can save your life, and other ones I can't remember. The Earth is flat because that suits capitalism; I haven't figured out how. When I'm at Target and, say, I'm in the soup aisle, I try to guesstimate the calories. I calculate there are a thousand different cans of soup that on average are about 300 calories a can, so that's 300,000 calories, which is about I would say 85 or so pounds meant for someone's body, and that's just one solitary aisle and not a very caloric one. So many calories, so who are they meant for? Perhaps calories fall off the edges of Earth. When I was a girl, I believed every product the factory made was good for me, so I accept you, Flat Earth. Each age needs its revisions and its mass hysterias. In 1726 Mary Toft convinced people she had given birth to rabbits, an improbable scenario a lot of people believed. Also, crop circles. If we're revising, I'd like to make some propositions: along the edge, sirens sing their hypnosis onto the rocky cays. You see water is endless because the edge is an infinite pool. On my Flat Earth, I walk on the surface of the ocean wielding a CGI trident and spouting the truth that feels best. What is seeing, I ask? A poet once told me I liked a theory of world I could aver with confidence. I'll live at the edge of the Earth where those next-world sirens write a form of poem called the sapphic that's made of drinking straws and seashell songs, despair, births, and conspiracy. We had a crisis of state, so along the edges we build a curve from the Earth into the galaxy, a renewal of her fertile potential.

TWO • Be Recorder

BE RECORDER

•

a monolith overshadows the animals
in their boxes stacked so corners stick
into corners of others for morale the animals
think about a next life while the monolith smothers
reality while a more necessary revolution awaits us
our shoes pinch made south in plastic forms
of animal skin layers of animal cells and the tiny
frays of thread meant to stitch shoes instead stitch
the lungs the fingers the stitches to fractions
of cents the kind of money to transform us all day
into new animals so how did I attain this onus
how do I break free of it or declare it my only trial
and what of the lying shark on the other
side of the door and his agenda like fill her hole
and shut her up and why insist on a skills test
that feels like gauntlet because my betters molding
me voice-over in megaphones stop thinking in the past
it's like shitting on the giant tapestry of the nation
since that really brings us *all* down emphasis theirs

•

I was light from the mouth from every part of me
I was of the earth or a scar in the earth pouring through
the ruins of early civilization and I bubbled from it and
became a saint's reptilian spirit and I could taste
the wheat and coal and gold that whiff of power
and I was vapor like a smog that becomes a wraith
over the city then back to animal form decompressed
and atomized into a past life as star and I was that animal
truth the spirit I had dreamt about being more cloud
and star than given I was just the density of water
a cycle in and out the fade of my fugitive
substance going south and the yearn for decadence
disappears in the annals yet leaves a taste in the mouth
metallic and lime the sense of dissolution and I was speed
and avowal to reset the orb of gravity I was risen from foam
necessitated by colony sired in violence exported as luxury

•

the animal   imagines   what life is   in her fiefdom
what the edges of her domain are
what parables   become policy
vice-versa the animal   susses out   confederate
from the horde   the animal defines the age's pathology
how   will the   animal cure it
how does the animal describe   its worry
and recognizing it   how does the animal
solve   the animal   outside of   time
does the animal   become an immunity
or serve   the fiefdom   what is the give
and   the takeaway   is it false hope
inescapable class   the fortune   a fortress
we all grew up   frozen to a tier
are we up or down or over

•

in the legion of animals
the serpent is the queen
and the elephant the serf
the microbe is the god and
the human animal is that
god's host the factory is
apex maw the folklore its
enforcer father is both lord
and rod and mother is
dollar-dollar bills
molten core of the real

•

I hardly care that I'm doing
harpy that I'm a city's pestilence
should I mother or write
serve art or the state

•

am I the monkey on the crocodile's back
or just a brown-winged dove and can
you modify art to suit my ample otherness
I know we're friends though I'm that friend
you tally on your list of goodwill for domesticating
my otherness but why is your gesture phoned-in
or scared to offend the august king who pretends
at false hope while denser evils dock in gated
communities built on imported bootstraps since
they can't repel our work corpses so how do we meet
halfway when the toll is steep and so is the road

•

I became American each time
my parents became American
each instance symbolizing a different
version of being American
first is when they decided to stay
and next is the photo of my parents beaming
by a judge with citizenship in their hand
also the photo of my mother and father
in the '60s looking like any American
perhaps foreign only in tongue
the Statue of Liberty behind them
or the first time they're registered
as American by having an American
job   though I was born in America
I wasn't born American
I know it's hard to understand
but it's also not hard I became American
when I memorized the national anthem
or when I had sex with a white boy
or when I thought my first
racist thought or when I decided
I wanted to always live in a place like US
which is how America becomes
an event that happens only for the lucky
so the question *where are you from* means I was born
foreign in America but not their America
I mean the chain of land called America connected
by chains of mountains where minute threads of
the first people who lived that America live in me
when there was the earth giving only over
what she wanted that was before she became American

•

how long I yearned
for a slice of the monolith's
throbbing global power
over all of me as well as
the you the thee the thou
the them and the us
in a tangle of want since
winter was coming he was
a giant wriggling worm
circling the earth leeching
human ore in the name
of God dressed as The Rock
encased in Mizrahi
for Target and straddling
the Golden Gate Bridge
in a 'roid rage battling the alien

brown bodies brown
murdered bodies and drowned
bodies brown repelled bodies
uncounted brown bodies
on borders in boats from hurricanes
in holds and shipping
containers against walls the new word
for global encroachment
and now winter

•

can I trust your simpatico or will my dark repel
will you be frontier and border kiss me for the camera
can I have authentic depth and will you align with me
will you hold my curls when I'm expelling phantoms
who open tunnels into the past will you consider the sky
contra the west with its grinding machines will you Spartacus
with me will you jump in and fight can it be your caravan too
record my face lover record my limbs record them for
us all I'm lucky I'm lucky I'm so lucky that I'm lucky

•

who leads this tango
the thief or the judge
the huckster or the king
can I trust the ardor
or is it just theater
will I be claimant or
defendant fool or shaman
animal or asset
plough or oxen
are we going to get
ahistorical because of
the inconvenience of the thing
disguised as the thing
that sounds like shrimperial
and rhymes with shrivilege
and is tinged with shrisease
I could just leave the grid
for exile but what island would
I become and how would
I still make interventions
into culture where might
I find the suitable therefore
inferior slot for me
could I live there for good
if I pay my taxes and how civil
would I have to perform
like arboretum or like
public statue of a settler
or like skate park or
recreation center
how would you evaluate
how I was or was not what you
hoped true and erotically
where should I plant

the old self because she's loose
and hot and deranged
riled and ill-tempered
can she be denatured
can she be defanged
can she be fauna
of the seventh dimension
how do I suppress my cynicism
when you tangle my money
with blood devour my glimmer
co-opt and whitewash
how do I build a home on sand
which map do I use
do I adapt to code to form
to tradition and where do I belong
shall I ask permission
do I beg for a license
that warrants my claim

•

why are we wedged   so much horchata
mulatta corbata pirata   and obvi piñata
metiste la pata   cuando abriste la boca
            pero te lo digo with love

•

am I the mariner
and whose bird was it
and how does absolution
work and are counter-
histories in your allusions
and am I your audience or
am I actually the one who louses
up the place a sign of the raptures
to come am I the false flag operation
of crisis actors in a San Mateo
high school down the way
from a #secession billboard
will I be reincarnated as elephant
as king as flea as barnacle
why am I the locus of your discontent
and not your president
your intimate the landlord
an aesthetic overlord
how do I hang from your neck
with such ease and when
will I be graced with immunity

•

the animal infiltrates the maze outside
the wall a whimper a moan the mewl
of the lamb bears the yoke of Assimilation
while our sweatshirts bear the logos of Ambition
the animal burrows under the monolith's base
the animal intercepts or plunders which is why
walls go deep into hell and out and up and down
until our throats are dusty with the grit
from the walls once I knew a man who thought
to prevent birds' migration the wall
should reach into the sky restrict the satellites
make the wall that reaches into space
constructed by the former middle
class who will learn how to make walls
from the wall-making app the government
mails them after The Great Obsolescence
that'll happen you know one day you're supreme
animal in the rainbow the next you're a mob's cog
patrolling a border and the next you're stacking bricks
imprinted with the Amazon flag just like your beloved
media-construct wanted for you and your
helpmates such pretty girls such soft hands

•

I'd once have left
brown behind
having already
left the tribe behind
and her tongue
and the garb that made me
theirs behind because it felt
like leaving hoi polloi behind
to finally put behind the chola
in my mother's tongue
lingering in quiet deep vowels
behind meant I could leave
behind inferiority complex
not really but in theory

I tried to leave my eden-dreams
behind but they stuck to my shoe

because of my anarchic spirit
I leave behind dignity
so the angel inside me
stays behind me too
along with my poison pen

never mind I'll need that

anger was my primary breathing
apparatus for so long
what a mixed blessing when it worked
I've learned the most from the cracked
once I broke into pieces
now I break into wholes

•

the hasty deportation wave of 2025
came via the dour pilgrim's burlap sack

he launched us into the river
on the edge of so-called civilization

and there was such a taste of afterlife
to the spell of fireworks
on that enchanting independence day

•

how much credit do I claim   and where do I claim it like at the office of art claims   or

the office of welfare and how   did I earn   contempt   was it   my cheeky   or

basic mode   I suffer how I suffer   and   it's all my fault   is there a grant   or

should I get an agent   in all senses of the word literary and   cultural and mask   or

will my class ascent   assuage your guilt   is it ever   inevitable   or

do I   remind you   of   the ilk   you find both offensive   and sexy   or

a manufactured monster   a caricature Chihuahua cubed   the token the share   or

a literal stranger at the   knights' table   does my hesitation   touch you   or

my affect   or my vision   or my gears   or my eternal indulgences   or

when it gets added up and tallied by the chamber whoever that is   and what I've earned   or

haven't earned   even then   even then   will I be   confirmation or inheritor

•

They built the US bunker in heaven
for the citizens who filled shelves
with formula guns toilet paper plates
and pallets of cans from Costco not just
for themselves but away from us
our bodies not supplicant enough
too marimacha not macho enuf bent coconut
too Black too much noisy too uppity
or like the saucy Univision talking head
who roasts oligarchs while the big network
reports on repeat that alien brown bodies
killed a woman in that haven San Francisco
and brown bodies put a baby
in a microwave in Missouri
and brown bodies loll by cacti
overteeming with a brown us
under a giant sombrero from Tijuana
and we all of us under the spell
of a new colonizing worm
construct hateful castes
sometimes wrongly in
an attempt to survive the boxes
how I could put my hips into it
like butterfly knives flicked out
of the pockets of the Xicana stereotypes
I aspired to while trying
preppie vowels the fraudulence of
belonging with my persona
still I survived and learned
to take each box apart
right to the cozy lap
of a college education
now I'm the thirteenth floor

•

I don't actually know who the richest
person I've ever known is and that's what
is so great about being an American and by
American I mean North American and by
North American I mean US and by US
I mean I'm a US citizen who may appear
to be rich to a lot of people so in a revolution
you can find me sleeping off my new status
hiding in a prison spoiler alert I believe in the state
in the end while the apocalypse roars outside

•

in another simultaneity
the end is corporate
in fire© and ice®
the meek go to work
because there is a workload
for the animal after death
she hurtles in deep space
where she can be a speck
of equal consequence
with the void

(after Pedro Pietri's "Puerto Rican Obituary")

•

they work their fingers
to the soul their bones
to their marrow
they toil in blankness
inside the dead yellow
rectangle of warehouse
windows work fingers
to knots of fire
the young the ancients
the boneless the broken
the warehouse does too
to the bone of the good
bones of the building
every splinter spoken for
she works to the centrifuge
of time the calendar a thorn
into the sole dollar of working
without pause work their mortal
coils into frayed threads until
just tatter they worked their bones
to the soul until there was no
soul left to send worked until
they were dead gone
to heaven or back home
for the dream to have USA
without USA to export
USA to the parts under
the leather sole of the boss
they work in dreams of working
under less than ideal conditions
instead of just not ideal
conditions work for the
shrinking pension and never
dental for the illusion

of the doctor medicating them
for work-related disease
until they die leaving no empire
only more dreams that their babies
should work less who instead
work more for less
so they continue to work
for them and their kin
they work balloon payment
in the form of a heart attack
if only that'll be me someday
the hopeless worker said on
the thirteenth of never
hollering into the canyon
of perpetual time
four bankruptcies later
three-fifths into a life
that she had planned
on expecting happiness
in any form it took
excluding the knockoff
cubed life she lived in debt
working to the millionth
of the cent her body cost
the machine's owner
Yolanda Berta Zoila
Chavela Lucia Esperanza
Naya Carmela Celia Rocio
once worked here
their work disappearing
into dream-emptied pockets
into the landfill of work
the work to make their bodies
into love for our own

•

when they revise the chronicles
the terms for naming us will
have to be something like
anational ones without the burden
of jingoism in a unique typeface
upper case optional
intended for topical use only
I'm willing to draft some
language to justify funding
an initiative for inscribing
our new title onto the landscape
just charge it to my race card

•

prose v poetry
poetry v nation-state
nation-state v my hoard
my hoard v the dog
the dog v the scorpion
the scorpion v dirt
dirt v lamictal
lamictal v ennui
ennui v blunder
blunder v debt
debt v defect
defect v fucking
fucking v instagram
instagram v art
art v weed
weed v night
night v the wimpy kid
the wimpy kid v disquisition
disquisition v testing
testing v parallelism
parallelism v your textual surface
your textual surface v a glare
a glare v balm
balm v heat
heat v talking
talking v getting
getting v the diurnal clock
the diurnal clock v semester
semester v my tender spirit
my tender spirit v twaddle
twaddle v our wreckage
our wreckage v diagnosis
diagnosis v committee
committee v postfeminism

postfeminism v perimenopause
perimenopause v sentimentality
sentimentality v television
television v us
us v apple
apple v family
family v flight
flight v the bourgeoisie
the bourgeoisie v torpor
torpor v sunshine
sunshine v your company
your company v my duplicity
my duplicity v your ease
your ease v my programming
my programming v your door
your door v my puddles
my puddles v progeny
progeny v prose

•

do you remember
the different world
you wanted for your children
glowing like a nominally capitalist eden
and how good it felt to want the future
a little less glutted with money
because in those days
we wanted to uncover
and overturn I remember
thinking it would be another
world even better than the world
made by the greatest generation
sometimes so much better
I was sure I couldn't even imagine
all of the ways it would be better
esp. knowing this new world lived
in the edges of my imagination
and required connections into
other people's edges
to make the whole world new
and raw and hazy but delicious
deeply in the marrow
like the idea of Whitman
or the snowy surface
of the Virgin Mary filling me
with hope when God was clouds
and I was a young naïve nativist
back then when immigration
fueled the fantasy
however improbable in ways we
didn't know but 100% sure
we expected and back then I was
sure believing that time's march forward
begat progress vis-à-vis US we would

make it better for everyone
then the they conceptualized
how the idea of a once-better world
would profitably merch hope
and those robber baron's dollar bills
popped around like a halo
and the they sold the latest gadget
as panacea as lifestyle as campaign
turning our hungry edges into an Oz
machine for printing money
so now we have less than our illusion
less than progress only dregs and
the machine of that illusion emitting
toxins that's the most recent thing

•

but mommy made me to disrupt
at the hem of her apron weighed down
by the coin of her labor she sold her grace
for tips those days when you could
subsistence live off coins or live almost
a whole lifetime thinking your children
would be lawyers not a why-tress
rocket not candle so for her I hone
myself into a thorn in the giant's hand

•

we smear the map
with pungency you want
to swab us but you can't
making us more terrifying
we coagulate and compound
into a virulent fetid stream
bisecting your dreams
we're those who aren't there
this land made us
old phantoms

•

phantoms in the pantry
and from the pylon
and hiding in the cricks
of history or Arnold's
phantom of yourself
the *West Side Story*
phantom and the phantom
of sisters gone over
the phantom of long-lost moods
dense with speechlessness
the phantoms of squashed ants
and the off-course cricket's dirge
phantom dream trapped in your pillow
the despair of these phantoms
squared into bigger phantom
splatter of phantoms against the spray
their shadows above your bed
phantom vessels in the sea's hold
the phantom of streaks in the window
phantom of that recollection
Aragon's *abstract phantom*
phantom sister
why hast thou split
into a cavalcade of phantoms
for thou is purest idiom
in my arsenal phantom
infection clotting history
with tattered machination
the phantom of insistence
living there in the bedroom
and again in the kitchen the master's
spirit in the body's fleshy ghost

•

Miss America from sea to shining sea
the huddled masses have a concern
there is one of you and all of us

•

I play anchorbaby-opportunist-influx
and traffic my knack for accents and affects and for narrating
childhood fraudulence into artworks
and late at night I vanish into
teacher mother housekeeper
because who am I but a vortex of all those
personas contra class traitor semi-invisible
and forced into a figure defined by hurtling
into ascension   the past the present the lie
the reality the parlor game the miniseries
the battle older than me in my helix

•

the animal in the room hisses
and bucks and her boom
squeezes the whole foundation
squeezing all the words out
they twirl a piñata of George
Washington's head over the animal
it's filled with grenades of pomp
and fake outrage just like the good old '90s
when the animal wrongly learned
to avert her eyes tho she eventually
disobeyed which led to pain and regret
lo que no mata engorda
you may have heard that's
what some did with it

•

and how did trifling bureaucracies
lodge such   a vast
root   in me

I forget   my real vocation
not executive
not supplicant but
stepping back into daughterhood

rehearsing insolence to blank walls
the nay vote   of the   master's discontent
regaining consciousness
inside of a bullet

•

in my revisionist chronicle
a cabal of my favorite womxn
run the show their hair a wild
network of electricity charging
the new grid and the categories of today
consigned to a container shot into earth's
belly then cleave again and again into
a giant ovum blood burst in the marrow
of time a throbbing fold because it is
all the body in fecundity and some
switch restores connection and
that's as far as I get each time
it's a stunning light to see tho

•

isn't progress
such a chore when it's
for the other tribe
sisters and brothers
progress is also
the sledgehammer
for all monolith work
one brick at a time

•

how shall we remind the mathematicians
the politicians and the statisticians
and the megachurch man
and the gentrifying house-flipper
and the executive-garbage people
who hiked up the cost of Daraprim
and EpiPen and the Ponzi scheme
of senator-lobbyists and the propagandists
and the executive branch-corporate shills
and the patriarchal misogynist statesmen
and the Tiki torch-khakis boys
how shall we remind them that want is
the conduit aversion the trick card and
capital is the rabies and impulse
is the fuel that drives it we reject getting
jostled on currents or dismissed by judges
or reduced to hot pepper or into migrant
effigy or dismembered on borders
and razed by the US appetite
for Sinaloan meth in teeny baggies
with skulls on them each a real
human head tossed to the furrowed canals
edging our border lined with the bodies
of journalists and mayors a magical realism
not seen in your mediating literature

when do we stop layering with just post post post
make it the gel we're in   will it have
only symbolic heft or displace our bodies
because of the cannibal factory
releasing only one xenotype at a time free
with purchase of one million shiny objects

shall we write our demands in blood
with our histories cures mythologies curses
or should we develop a victor-approved
version of history how do we transform
their powers do we break them apart
and bury them set them on the shelf
do we push them out on the ice floe or take
away their scepters can we disrupt it
with our word parades or do we let them in
on the plot or do we burn them

●

I have to prepare to live tight and court danger
prepare to live on air I have to stop buying
and watching have to learn to turn hate
into light and uncover I think
dance to disco from the '70s oil crisis

I have to pull my money
out of the faux middle-class race

I'm separated from my nation
have to teach the kids to turn
off the lights to compost shoot a gun
and make agitational film
resist the lure
they will have to be tougher
so I have to mine for toughness
for me for the children
for their middle age
to accept it was long-coming
long con

tears are blood
act accordingly

have to overlook my invented
horizontal rival remember urgency
have to live against the wall
into the future into the disturbance
have to return to a marrow
of language I have to refuse to be
what they are to be what they'll do
will avenge will disturb
revise and filter don't want to
still have to

•

this new disturbance
could gather volition
and mass humanist buy-in
where I am alone and alert
where I've thickened my soul
by a severe scare quotes
artist mastermind installed
by the state to keep us docile
and ashamed which we do for
a hot second then stop and
become presumptuous even while
circled by junkyard dogs if it stops us
we are weak if it shapes us we
are what they name us

•

what is your origin   where did you suffer   what is your affinity group
how are you acquainted with industry   what will you bring to our guild
what are the qualities of a good serf   what is your mission in life
and could you sell me this instance   what is the last pornography that repulsed you
can you talk about   your research into the unsolvable   how would you
feign a diverse audience is a reader a client   did customers occur to you
as an outcome   what are three positive strains in you   does content
drive you into the market   does blunder drive you to work on a regular basis
when can you start with selective memory   is this the racket you had planned
was this your natal force   are you an open boomtown   or a care professional
what animal rules the roost   does that animal work as aphorism
pure revelation   or dispatch from the front lines   where is the monolith's fortress
and who is its benefactor   have you made anything good with our outrage
or built an endless abstract war   will an underclass hunger   qualify for your attention
or will you have to track down   their legitimacy yourself   can I expect
a chronicle   of the moment or is it fraught with the lyric   therefore fraught
with the vulgar density of   people is that the hitch   aesthetically
thus ethically   does it seem impossible   the desire for such validation
or could you   break free and record   be recorder

•

let's admit to our own complicity release into
the wound because imagine it's like a rose

blossom of scarred red tissue not beautiful
but layers and layers of lesions

layered over with more scar then more wound
over it and the edges are brittle from years

and years of wounding can you see it red white
purple orange yellow milk tears blue black

the colors of everywhere so why can't
we circle the wound all of us circle

it with balms and prayer with linked hands
around it a common song in Esperanto for instance

the resurgence of babel but as one braided
bellow the rope that leads to heaven

rousing the wound which could vibrate
and diminish into lesser scar a release like opening

a fist of morning glory but of broken skin like
a giant fractal spreading across the ice

it would be the end of one era the beginning
of another like the end of money or the end

of time except more difficult or impossible tho we
wouldn't televise or at least no commercial breaks

we'd be taking off the masks and
once they were off and some folks might finally

be in the seats we dreamt of when plotting
this insurrection against the wound and for

the animal   the fiefdom might have been your aunt's
or your father's and we apologize for disrupting

lineage but from where I sit the seas and the deserts
and islands are the source from which my sisters

and brothers ascend in their ceaseless
force and filled with light you go first then

I'll follow you say it and I'll repeat it and you will
repeat it and yours and mine and ours

will repeat it and it'll become the human drone
over the world that trembles out the clouds

tumbles them to wash over the cities wash
out our mouths the consonance draining out

into the sewers of our historical consciousness
and the new city rises from the bits of what

was the letters are shaped like us

THREE • Birthright

IN REMEMBRANCE OF THEIR LABORS

What is the nature of the brown artist's desire for disruption? My legacy: a long lineage of fuck-up hustlers, mostly on my father's side. On my mother's side: civil servants: three generations of accountants for the state. On my father's: scamps, scam artists, pimps, criminals: perfect models for destabilization.

From all sides: studious and intense labor, relentless work, under-the-table exchange.

I'm a node of various dark and light powers, first generation emitting energy from the first world. In remembrance of their labors, honest and corrupt, I infiltrate the creative class by squatting in its traditions.

This in remembrance of my impetuous mother and father's jet plane ride into the '60s maelstrom, and bussing tables and a tiny apartment in the Bronx and knowing only the English words for all-things-restaurant. I serve thee for thine labor is my staircase.

The frivolity of poetry, layers of frivolity disguised as labor or vice versa. Poetry is useless until we rot from inside when we don't have words.

Emancipatory lyric poetry. Deregulated lyric poetry. Lyric poetry with workboots. The lyric poetry of garbage, of kitsch, of Marianism, of cockroach and placenta and dirty fingernails. In remembrance of their very deep-kneed and hand-gnarling labors, I declare the ocean Latinx, its blue surface the tongue of our abuelas forming the rough syllables of our Americanized ideals.

In remembrance of my father's belief in text, the house filled with books of striving. I devour the argot of the oppressor and US opened me in *How to Win Friends and Influence People*. My favorite story was about the boy who befriended a czar who then married the boy's mother. It told me there would be a game.

This is in remembrance of my mother whose hands were callused against heat, biceps bulging from hauling vacuum cleaners and trays of grand slams.

Mercy to my failures and the legacy of failures beneath the surface of the heroic immigrant story I wish I was telling.

The public spectacle is cracking up and forth through the cracks we've made over the years: an ooze of new self.

In homage to different models of discourse, particularly the work of my pantheon: Gloria Anzaldúa, Cherríe Moraga, bell hooks, Ana Mendieta, Christina Sharpe, Audre Lorde, June Jordan, Lucille Clifton, Jessica Hagedorn, Patssi Valdez, Chela Sandoval, Emma Pérez, and Ana and also Mimi, Coco, Elvita, Monica and Cany, Zoilita Espe, Amalia. Las Claudias, Cristy.

Whiteness claims affective normativity and neutrality, but for that fantasy to remain in place one must only view it from the vantage point of US cultural and political hegemony. . . . This game is rigged insofar as it is meant to block access to freedom to those who cannot inhabit or at least mimic certain affective rhythms that have been preordained as acceptable. From the vantage point of this national affect code, Latina/o affect appears over the top and excessive. José Esteban Muñoz

I write in remembrance of all the nosotros muffled by the clang of dishes and jokes about Latinos. Why do Hispanics have small steering wheels? So they can drive with handcuffs on. What is the difference between a Hispanic and an elevator? One can raise a child. The connections of how certain formalisms erase so-called selves. The truth is that these so-called subjectivities are already translucent.

The context for the twenty-first-century Latina lyric I is an overfull rocket, a plate of entrails on my head. It is that I will stomp and duende, that I wear stiletto-knife chanclas. My peerless bosom is made of parrot feathers. This I is the guns and gang tattoos gallery for the visitors at the zoo. They call me Bullet.

I am in conclusion, a fracaso, a wreck of great consequence, and this will be like my prison tattoo. La Wrecking Crew. The resistance in this expression is therefore disruptive or pathetic intentionally or unintentionally.

To the future flor de cancion, innovator, and disturber of the story, I say, coalesce and rise. Destroy. In remembrance: kick and scream para el carajo.

AS BODY II

The soul needs
no self-reference
she's busy producing
pleasure and moral reason
holding us upright

yet we endure so many
tricks when all we want is
the tang of touching
or the verve we felt
when we still shone
with that hope called naïveté
in response my soul
improvises another carnal
extravaganza that I record
because I like all notions
mocked as a thicket
of syrupy thuds
or as no longer germane
soul *qua* soul say

the more tenuous risk
        is soul
which some leave behind
dusty in the back of an old
flaking book a sibylline song
drawing me in not like
a bearded god in the clouds
but traces and tones and slithering
vapors a metaphysical Cheshire
telling me I could finally evict
the angry fist who became chairman
        of me for some time

I don't blame him
I was being permeable

today my soul is a deflated balloon
hissing her air out falling up and onto
sky's wetted lips where the birds urge
      fly little soul fly

so imagine all of your bodily urges
crying out at once
then suddenly the borders
of everyone
blur into one hot mess
bleeding breathing learning
drinking stabbing
golding dying milking
stroking digging

glistening gesturing
shaking bounding staining
chasing greening
punking dittoing
barricading and working it
levitating cheating clouding
defending depressing lying

in return that dimension
without sensibility
where my soul
falls into a crevasse of data
for the future to find

spitting sicking
adhering framing furring
alabastering fretting
snorting lulling
solipsizing not getting past
the beginning

I WILL BE MY MOTHER'S APPRENTICE

as if I were a hunger because
it is our bleak and common future
to reverse the sphinx. I study the meander
of her logic for context. Sometimes it is
like a poem that is not quite realized
filled with hollows and bursts,
a stranger's grief and rage. She asks
for home when she's home. She screams
for the purse we haven't hidden from her.
Sometimes we circle the same spots,
and I try to be as I know she was with me
once: remedy and anchor. I'm a fair
to poor replica, yet still her proxy.

That you didn't know her is your
misfortune: a hot planet's core,
late summer's best light. As metaphor
I evoke a pink, vulnerable jelly,
translucent and containing the past.
I hold it in my hand and against a lamp.
This is our intimacy now. My nails trace
the brown spots that mark her losses.
Beautiful and sad and strange, I say,
because I've made her into something else.

BEASTS

My siblings and I archive the blanks in my mother's memory,
diagnose her in text messages. *And so it begins*, I write although

her disease had no true beginning, only a gradual peeling away
until she was left a live wire of disquiet. We frame her illness

as a conceptual resistance—*She thinks, yet she is an other*—
to make sense of the shift. She forgot my brother's cancer,

for example, and her shock, which registered as surprise,
was the reaction to any story we told her, a peak of sublimity

over and over. Once on a walk she told us she thought
she was getting better. Exhausted, we told her she was incurable,

a child's revenge. Her flash of sorrow was tempered only
by her forgetting and new talk of a remedy,

and we continued with the fiction because darker dwindling
awaited us like rage, suspicion, delusion, estrangement.

I had once told myself a different story about us;
in it she was a living marble goddess in my house

watching over my children and me, so what a bitter fruit
for us to share, our hands sinking into its fetid bruise,

the harsh flavor stretched over all our days, coloring them gray,
infesting them with the beasts that disappeared her,

beasts that hid her mail in shoeboxes under her bed,
bills unpaid for months, boxes to their brims. The lesson:

memory, which once seemed impermeable, had always been
a muslin, spilling the self out like water, so that one became

a new species of naïf and martyr. And we're made a cabal
of medieval scholars speculating how many splinters of light

make up her core, how much we might harvest before
she disappears. This is the new love: us making an inventory

of her failing body to divide into pieces we can manage—
her shame our reward, and I'll speak for the three of us:

we would have liked her to relish in the boons that never came,
our own failures amplified by her fading quality.

ENTANGLEMENT

We love what's best in our beloved, what's worst in them.
You have to like what time does. Each day I talk to the part
of me that is my beloved from a tiny telephone in me.
I communicate in the clicks and beeps of our abbreviated tongue.
Love is a long trial, a wending, and an uneven effort.
I hate the word faith, but that's all there is. Only
the last one standing knows the score. Think of the types
of violence on a continuum, and toward the mildest
end is love. *I'm torn by you!* I scream when my beloved
pulls at our bond. I'm an alien host or we are two yous
subsumed by a single body. The beloved says, *You changed
my brain; and I am at that mercy*, which is meant
as a warranty for longevity, but there is no real promise:
you keep knowing each other and knowing each other.

AMERICAN MYTHOS

My son leaves me a Post-it on the lamp asking me to email Amazon about the *Star Wars* video game. He gave me the money and I lied about ordering it. I hadn't even clicked.

Star Wars is the first time I saw space's mien. Space swallowed the whole theater and it smelled of soldering, and brake pads, and gold. Vast and unknowable, it could crush me like the ocean.

I tell him a story about a delay in a Denver warehouse, then played out the lie to myself all night: my writing Amazon to add texture to the lie, then the laying off of said Amazon warehouse worker in roller blades, then that worker's nightmare of applying for unemployment. The worker's body is destroyed by that labor, yet he only has an infinitesimal chance of collecting workman's comp. All of this chaos spurred by my inertia and white lies.

I feel shame, but not propulsive enough to spur an actual login. Does this paralysis have a name?

I suffer from anxiety over pulling the trigger, extending a finger into the chill of network, baring my economic thorax. I want to buy the game for him; I don't want to participate in the economy; I don't have the money; he is mouthy; I am weak; I am lazy. He will be sucked into the game and become a criminal or the sounds of the game will invade my dreams. The game brainwashes him for a future war against my kind.

I read the reviews for the video game, almost drop it into the virtual cart, but I can't end the transaction. Answering email, paying bills, all of it freezes me.

•

I vacillate about the game because of all the death in it. *Star Wars* doesn't have spurts of blood but depicts the random murder of young men in Rebel X-Wings who have families waiting for them on their respective planets.

I had so long coasted on the moral pleasure of sadistic and feudal Minecraft, but spacescapes are first-world adolescence. By having a humanist ethos, might I be denying my boy a type of survival in the world ahead? He would stumble with a gun in his hand and shoot himself, disfigure his beautiful face.

If I were my father, I would buy my son the game and also a new video game system and a new TV that covers the entire wall. I would buy him a real gun and take him out to shoot at mailboxes and birds, all on a credit card I would default on because America.

•

It was night, and I almost ordered the game, until I froze because of all boys, and because of my hungers that replicate what the screens tell me. I lock my doors. My son's small rages. A young man with the world not in his hand, the wrong voice in his head telling him someone was always trying to take something that belonged to him.

I offer my son books, but their ancient codex system makes no sense to him. I have piles of books around me. Mostly they are for my selfies and so that I can feel at home in knowledge. The books become doorstops, they become relics.

In a few years my son might be watching beheading videos on the Internet and getting inured like when I saw the *Time* magazine cover with the dead bodies laid side by side at Jonestown. Flies swarmed their bodies covered with white sheets that barely hid their face. I was seven.

•

My boy is an exquisite synergy of the colonizer and the colonized: the round face with a smattering of freckles, the fair skin and the narrow toes. His white skin makes him a mutable force of power in any room. His intensity is not an errant trait. It is his two parents' histories refracted and exploded into mercenary biologies. And in an apocalypse, how will his children survive? My cousin's husband teaches his boys to wrestle, holds their arms. *Fight for your life*, he orders them, nudging them to a core instinct of the brain. Their will activated, the boys struggle to escape their father's thick arms. The world is ugly. There will be terrible humans, there always are. They will continue being terrible, so their father teaches them to fight. In my origin family, this is what we do.

•

Another reason not to buy: Earth and shipping and the person who makes the airbags sent in a box shipped to a factory then promptly shipped back out on a plane only because I want to save 43 cents or the trip to the sad, abandoned mall. The world is too much and keeps me in the house, ordering it all in.

•

Someday my son's children will play the games projecting virtual bodies into the room, and the children that follow them will play with bodies that smell like they are in the room. Then the children that follow: no bodies at all, just the pulse of adrenaline from the limbic system and into the central nervous system that may or may not be a set of wires connected to gelatin and a solar panel.

•

Mom, he whispers, his voice trembling.
Yes, I answer sternly.
Never mind, he replies, miserable with impotence.

•

So say time passes and I get older and older. I get close to seventy, but I wouldn't know or remember. Time goes on into the future, which is becoming increasingly darker. Meanwhile, my son goes on to have a life affected marginally by *Star Wars*, and more generally by the psychodynamic he grew up in, which is, more or less, average bougie child with a kid sister, narcissistic parents, and ecological disaster.

And then many years later, I die of a disease brought on by the violence I laid at my door. The Spanish hands and quick wit I inherited from my mother come laden with the shittiest disease in the universe. I'm talking about the future without my body, but first the brain goes in little chips like mica shedding memory and volition at random—simultaneously.

My son, now older, would have memories of me, of what I was, of what I had been, but more importantly, the lessons of *Star Wars*. I made myself an American who would mention my exoticisms in stories: my inability to use the word "clothes" correctly, for example, how loud my voice was, the weird, insulting nicknames.

The world will worsen. Meanwhile, *SW*™ virtual reality glasses turn people into any character in the movies, even the minor ones, and eventually there is a jelly a mega-fan can smear on her body to feel the viscera of *Star Wars* called *SWTranscendia*. Then everyone wants that and water and food too, so the world ends.

The boot-on-neck people will like telling us we won't survive over the speakers in the Google vans that record our every gesture, and we lose human decency month after month. As time goes by, we create an escape route out of our house, bury canned foods in the desert.

•

In the future, *Star Wars* is woven into a macro-projection of the present and the past; history's crumbling bedrock is built of figments like always, but occupied massive blocks of data that, in this new age, are not sustainable.

After the end of the world's lineage, my son is an elder who passes down the stories the television once told him: the flat living characters were sent through light and a poor man would invade your house and take your things or take your identity, which is numbers. In the distant past, there were television shows about surviving the apocalypse; its protagonist, the implacable and heroic white father. The distinction between fiction and nonfiction blurred.

We eat the paint off paintings when we become desperate or all that art vanishes under a torrent, into a volcano, down a fault line. High art gives way to the drone of nationalist exposition blaring from public address speakers.

We will have to rediscover some knowledge while, in another universe, they have already found ways to not have bodies.

•

The storytellers that survive pass *Star Wars* to other generations by talking or gesticulating. My lineage survives and they weave threads of *SW* into their new languages like the walking rug and the muppet toad-man who passes on wisdom and embodied physical arts. The interior of the stars that live above the hundreds of fogs is other people fighting to save us. *SW* becomes a story helix. People treasure the artifacts that helped illustrate the story, like a Stormtrooper action figure left in vaults by prescient scholars, or an AT-AT, the tale's Trojan Horse, the ass carrying the virgin through the galaxy.

Another part of the mythology spread across the end of the Americas: in those days the king was a black foreign usurper from a black planet because a narrative like that always survives.

Lucky for us the failure of the grid blips out their bile, like a high colonic for the earth. Everything burned, or text is no longer matter, so no fire required. A grid failure. Surely the world and some human inhabitants find some stasis, however brutal. The stasis is informed by lore about civilization.

•

I should buy my son the video game to transport him to some humanist sublimity with meditation or self-improvement and deadly aim, but I order the *Star Wars* game and, accidentally, a book on Pilates, a book on organizing, and eyeliner, the virtual items I had left in the virtual cart on one of my aspirational Amazon shopping sprees.

In my conscience I justify the game as an exchange for a little compliance, insurance against being set loose upon a metaphorical ice floe into the stars alone.

•

That night, my son couldn't sleep because he had been obsessing over my mother's decay which was so florid, dead and not dead, and this was the affront to him, that we all become nothing, and that bit by bit, being gets taken away from all of us.

His entire life represented only a quarter of mine, a fragment of my mother's.

But we also have life. I held his body tight to mine so we were two, dying and living. In his body were all the forms he would take, promise and rot. Someday he would also scrutinize my dying, parse it out for his children or his beloved.

We sat in the darkness and quiet or maybe the eddy the words created. *I'm crying, mama*, he said, *but these are tears of joy.*

•

In the future, they endure for however long they can. They endure wordlessly and into many generations, each one losing its will after being ground down because almost all people are ground down, a privilege to be fresh-eyed for eternity.

Once there were swords, they would say, that made the sound of empty oil drums. Once there was a ship powered by bones that flew in the air without moving a single feather, which they had never seen. Feathers were like hair.

ON TEACHING

The coils from me to her to them
to him like when we project words
as matter temporal
or not knowing
what they were but sound
                    Those branches
still pulse with the plasma of exchange

        a song between us
and the imbalance we tried
        languidly to invert because
it was ancient I tried? I didn't try
        though it was on me?

        We said to each other give me
your attention or a haunting We invented
        categories of invention We asked what
the I could be today or we'd drop the I in history
        all of us with our contrary certainty

The old contacts and old contracts
        feel keen in my guts
My not-children my teachers
        mine mine mine

TERMINAL HAIR

On the edge of a mountain in Santa Fe
my friend and I talk about how we get rid of body
hair and what it was like when we were young,
and how we don't care as much as we used to,
and how our virility has drawn lovers to us.
Now some of our hairs come in coarse and white as
an old man's beard. We speculate our moustaches
connect us to a remote ancestress whose moustache
was denser than ours when having a moustache
was a little easier and this legacy
softens the blow because name one actress
or model or singer or female celebrity
with a moustache. There's that photo of Madonna
and her hairy armpits. Frida Kahlo was foreign
and transcendent so pardoned, but no one else.
The ancestress we imagine never married, or she had
lover after lover. They called her Bigote or Takachu
or La Baffi. Nobody said a word about it because they
were scared to or she lived on the edge of the town
where she was left alone and didn't care.
Maybe she found herself a good-natured companion
who stroked her moustache and nipped at it
or shaped it with soap, and at some point
later in her life she said to herself, someday
my great-great-great-great granddaughters
will stand on a cliff and survey their vast terrains,
the wind bristling the hair above their lips.

ONLY A SHADOW

My daughter gathers the seeds she finds in our desert, calls them
spirits. *The spirits are us*, she says while I knead the orbs in my fingers

to call up her birth. The wind's first thought is to free those seeds:
vessels of the tree's worry that she's not enough of a multiplicity,

that she will burn into the cosmos. The cosmos is no thought, no worry,
more than us, but less than wind, and the wind is only the infinite,

not the body's death, which is, after all, only a particle, but time as formless
as space. This is only if the wind worries at all. The seed doesn't think;

she is the doubling ambition of a vessel. In the wind, the idea
of the copy is translated by time. We were once that idea. My daughter

collects me in a box marked for spirits where I unsettle the other seeds
begging for wind so that my sound will echo a thousand miles away.

My daughter is now the pulse I toss into the wind with the seeds. Particles
of us pass over like whispers through the cosmos, upon the clatter

the wind makes. I worry that when birds take her into themselves,
she'll become a fleck of their transience, but this is how we permeate

the cosmos, the twine of our breaths into wind, into carbon,
into the tree's colossal fingers reaching back from inside the earth.

ARS POETICA

I'm ill   I'm federal   I'm on leave   I'm a child of refuge   I'm holy   I'm a shit
I'm desperate   I won't tell you anything   I'm first-gen   I'm Gen X   I'm tied up
I'm bipolar   I'm   not fertile   I'm a secret   I'm the now
I'm indifferent I'm a disgrace   I'm funny   I'm assistance   I'm not saved
I was Mormon I'm atheist   I'm mysterious   I'm scared   I'm head of household
I'm quick-tempered   I'm day job   I'm night-ghost I'm failure   I act white
I   live bankrolled I'm deliverable   I'm not gang   I'm   crazy ex   I'm
slippery   I'm post-post-post   I'm   greedy   I'm double-crossing   I'm delusional
I'm above average BMI I'm hairy   I'm indebted I'm weak   I'm non-confrontational
I'm in therapy I'm sorry   I'm empowered   I don't have a tattoo   I don't have money
I have too many ex-friends   I'm agoraphobic   I'm recorder
I   have a valid passport   I've never been arrested   I should have been arrested
I know too much   I can barely read at times   I can barely rise at times
I'm gay   I'm marginally fit   I'm arthritic   I'm flaky
I have few skills   I'm salty   I'm a time bomb
I'm baptized   I'm dry   I'm chronic pain   I'm big at mom's house
I can't remember how many   I am obstructionist   I'm a Master
That was my   confessional   Thank you   very   much

NOTES

The lines attributed to Violeta Parra are from her song "Gracias a la Vida."

Pedro Pietri's "Puerto Rican Obituary" is a seminal work of Latinx poetry and can be found in his *Selected Poetry*, published by City Lights Books in 2015.

The José Esteban Muñoz quote in "In Remembrance of Their Labors" is excerpted from his essay "Feeling Brown: Ethnicity and Affect in Ricardo Bracho's *The Sweetest Hangover (and Other STDs)*."

The poem "Only a Shadow" was written for the Pintura/Palabra project sponsored by Letras Latinas. The poem is after the photograph *¿Sola Una Sombra? Only a Shadow (Ester IV)?* by Muriel Hasbun.

ACKNOWLEDGMENTS

Poems and prose published in this book have appeared in: *The Baffler*, *Boston Review*, *Colorado Review*, *Cream City Review*, *Fence*, *The Georgia Review*, *Harper's*, *Lit Hub*, *Mandorla*, *Omniverse*, *Ostrich Review*, *Other Musics: Latina Poetry*, *P-Queue*, PEN.org, *Pleiades*, Poem-A-Day at poets.org, *Poetry*, *The Rumpus*, *Southern Indiana Review*, *Syncretism & Survival: A Forum on Poetics*, and *Washington Square Review*.

Jeff Shotts is one of the best editors around, and I'm so grateful to him for helping me see all the possibilities in this book. I also want to thank J. Michael Martinez for always being a champion and for being the catalyst by asking me to write a poem about Latinidad and for being my Lil Keats and my brother. Special thanks to Krystal Languell who helped me see "Be Recorder" as a long poem and for being my longtime comrade in poetry. Dana Levin made the poems' endings so much better and her good spirit always guides me. Stephanie Burt's incredible attention to sound and sense also changed this book for the better, as did her friendship and eggy advice. Suzi, you're my rock. Thanks for keeping me sane by being so full of life and love.

I dedicate this book to my very dearest Mark Wunderlich who has also been my brother, my hero, and my partner-in-art-and-wickedness.

I am grateful for the time to write I received from CantoMundo, the Hermitage Foundation, the Howard Foundation, and the Blue Mountain Retreat.

To the teacher/mentors/guides/heroes and always-friends and inspirations: Elmaz Abinader, Francisco Aragon, Mary Jo Bang, Marvin Bell, Virginia de Araujo, Forrest Gander, Rigoberto Gonzalez, Juan Felipe Herrera, Brenda Hillman, Barbara Neilsen, Aldon Nielsen, Margarita Luna Robles, Nathan Sheehy, and Alan Soldofsky.

I'm so grateful for my family: to Evan Lavender-Smith for reading many drafts of this long poem and helping me find the time to write it and for kind and enduring support. Jackson and Sofia, my brother Jorge and sister Monica and little Liam. Thank you to Gail Lavender, Barry Smith, and Mark Whitehead, and Jordan and Yael Lavender-Smith, Luly and Sam. Zoila Roselló, Esperanza Roselló, Coco Roselló. For Cany and Gabe and Adrian and Brandon Barron, Yolanda Roselló, Elva Rosenfeld, Claudia and Cristi Carhuayo.

And to the friends and watersoul-family who helped with this book directly or indirectly: Gina Abelkop, Rosa Alcalá, Emily Alex, Diana Arterian, Jessie Bennett, Courtney Blaskower, Sara Borjas, Daniel Borzutsky, Jenny Boully, Susan Briante, Tisa Bryant, Jack Bunting, Anthony Cody, Carolina Ebeid, Lauren Espinoza, Adam Fitzgerald, Todd Fredson, Richard Greenfield, Camille Guthrie, Juan Luis Guzmán, Sarah Gzemski, Rachel Haley Himmelheber, Lily Hoang, Eunsong Kim, Ruth Ellen Kocher, Gloria Macijewski, Dawn Lundy Martin, Farid Matuk, Erika Meitner, Celeste Mendoza, Veronica Montes, Yesenia Montilla, Dawn Murphy, Mirna Palacio Ornelas, Andrea Orzoff, Jack Owens, Deb Paredez, Khadijah Queen, Dylan Retzinger, Barbara Richardson, Joe Rodriguez, Lucinda Roy, Dominique Salas, Amy Sayres-Baptista, Sandra Simonds, giovanni singleton, Tony Stagliano, Craig Morgan Teicher, Roberto Tejada, Naima Woods Tokunow, Aïda Torresola, Sarah Vap, Madeline Vardell, Rachelle Wales, Claire Vaye Watkins, Justine Wells, and Magdalena Zurawski.

My love to Soham Patel.

CARMEN GIMÉNEZ SMITH, nacida en Bronx, New York, EEUU, y hija de un Argentino y una Peruana, has lived in New Jersey, Maryland, Northern and Southern California, Iowa, New Mexico, and Mexico City. She is a queer poet and editor who currently lives in Blacksburg, Virginia, where she is a Professor of English in Virginia Tech's MFA program in creative writing. She received her BA in English from San Jose State University and her MFA from the University of Iowa. She is founder of Noemi Press and, with Stephanie Burt, poetry editor at the *Nation*. She has received fellowships from the Guggenheim Foundation, the Howard Foundation, and the Hermitage Foundation. She is the author of six collections of poetry including *Cruel Futures* and *Milk and Filth*, a finalist for the National Book Critics Circle Award. She is also the author of the lyric memoir *Bring Down the Little Birds*, which wc ι an American Book Award. A CantoMundo fellow, she now serves as a co-director.

The text of *Be Recorder* is set in Perpetua.
Book design by Rachel Holscher.
Composition by Bookmobile Design and Digital
Publisher Services, Minneapolis, Minnesota.
Manufactured by Versa Press on acid-free,
30 percent postconsumer wastepaper.